TAX SECRETS BEYOND THE TRADES

Stock Market Tax Mastery

By

CA PANKAJ HIMTHANI

About The Author

CA Pankaj Himthani is a Chartered Accountant by profession and a passionate trader by heart. With a unique blend of expertise in Finance, taxation, and trading experience, Pankaj has become a go-to expert for stock market traders and investors seeking guidance on tax compliance and planning.

As a Chartered Accountant, Pankaj has spent years honing his skills in taxation, accounting, and financial planning. He has worked with numerous clients, including individuals, businesses, and corporations, providing them with customized tax solutions that meet their specific needs.

With years of experience in the financial domain, CA Pankaj Himthani understands the challenges faced by stock market participants regarding taxation. His in-depth knowledge of capital gains tax, income tax laws, and regulatory frameworks enables him to provide strategic tax solutions that optimize profits while ensuring full compliance.

However, Pankaj's true passion lies in trading. He has been an active trader for many years and has a deep understanding of the markets, trading strategies, and risk management techniques. This unique combination of taxation expertise and trading experience enables Pankaj to provide insightful guidance to traders and investors on tax-related matters.

Through this book, Pankaj aims to share his knowledge and expertise with a wider audience, providing stock market traders and investors with the tools and insights they need to navigate the complex world of tax compliance and planning.

CA Pankaj Himthani regularly publishes articles on various websites and is interviewed by moneycontrol.com on trading and tax planning.

WHY THIS BOOK? 

Pankaj wrote this book to fill a critical gap in the market. As a trader and tax expert, he realized that many stock market traders and investors were struggling to navigate the complex world of tax compliance and planning. This book provides a comprehensive guide to tax compliance and planning for stock market traders and investors, drawing on Pankaj's unique expertise and experience.

ABOUT THIS BOOK? 

"Tax Secrets Beyond the Trades"

Do you know 75% of stock market trader file their ITR wrong or non-complied?

As a stock market trader or investor, you know that making informed investment decisions is crucial to your success. However, navigating the complex world of tax compliances and planning can be overwhelming, even for the most experienced traders and investors.

"Tax Secrets Beyond the Trades" is the ultimate guide for stock market traders and investors looking to navigate the complexities of tax compliance and tax planning. Whether you're a day trader, swing trader, or long-term investor, understanding taxation is crucial to maximizing your profits and staying compliant with regulations.

This book unravels the **hidden tax secrets** that can help traders and investors legally minimize their tax liabilities while optimizing their financial strategies. It covers essential topics such as capital gains tax, intra-day and F&O taxation, deductions, exemptions, and tax-saving strategies tailored specifically for market participants.

With a practical and easy-to-understand approach, **"Tax Secrets Beyond the Trades"** empowers readers to:

- Decode tax laws relevant to stock market earnings
- Identify common tax pitfalls and how to avoid them
- Leverage tax-efficient strategies to boost wealth accumulation

- Stay compliant while optimizing tax savings

Written by **CA Pankaj Himthani**, a Chartered Accountant and passionate trader, this book bridges the gap between taxation and trading, ensuring that traders and investors make informed financial decisions.

Why This Book is Important:

Tax compliance and planning are critical components of successful stock market trading and investing. Failure to comply with tax laws and regulations can result in significant penalties and losses. "Tax Secrets Beyond the Trades" provides you with the knowledge and insights you need to navigate the complex world of tax compliance and planning and to achieve your financial goals.

Who This Book Is For

"Tax Secrets Beyond the Trades" is designed for anyone involved in the stock market who wants to understand the nuances of tax compliance and strategic tax planning. If you earn from trading or investing, this book will help you legally minimize your tax burden, maximize your profits, and achieve your financial goals.

This book is perfect for:

- Stock Market Traders – Whether you are a day trader, swing trader, or F&O trader, this book will guide you through tax implications, deductions, and compliance strategies tailored for active market participants.

- Long-Term Investors – If you invest in equities, mutual funds, or ETFs, understanding capital gains taxation and tax-saving opportunities is crucial for wealth accumulation.

- High-Frequency & Algorithmic Traders – Those involved in automated trading or high-volume transactions can benefit from learning how to structure their trades tax-efficiently.

- Tax Professionals & Financial Advisors – Accountants, CAs, and tax consultants can use this book as a reference guide to assist clients in trading-related tax compliance and planning.

- Beginners in the Stock Market – If you are new to trading or investing, this book will help you build a solid foundation in tax basics, preventing costly mistakes in your financial journey.

- Business Owners & Professionals Investing in the Market – If you trade or invest alongside your primary business or profession, this book will help you align your tax strategies for optimal financial growth.

By the end of "Tax Secrets Beyond the Trades," you will have a clear understanding of tax laws, compliance requirements, and proven strategies to legally reduce your tax liabilities while growing your trading and investment income. This book provides valuable insights, practical examples, and expert guidance to help you achieve your financial goals.

ACKNOWLEDGMENT 

With immense gratitude, I acknowledge the **Universe** for its infinite wisdom, guidance, and abundance. This journey of writing **"Tax Secrets Beyond the Trades"** has been filled with learning, growth, and purpose, and I firmly believe that everything has unfolded at the right time and in the right way. The unseen forces of the Universe have aligned opportunities, people, and knowledge to make this book a reality, and for that, I am truly thankful.

I extend my deepest gratitude to my **family** - My parents, Ashok Kumar Himthani & Manju Himthani, for instilling in me the value of hard work and perseverance. My wife, Jasmine Himthani, thank you for your unwavering support and encouragement throughout this project. My children, Adiva & Ayaan, thank you for their patience and understanding while

I spent long hours writing. My sister, Dr. Neelam & brother-in-law, Ravi Tewari, thank you for your unwavering support, patience, and belief in my vision. Their encouragement has been my greatest motivation throughout this journey.

A special thanks to my **mentors, colleagues, and fellow traders** who have shared their insights and experiences, helping me shape the practical approach of this book. Your valuable discussions and perspectives have greatly enriched my understanding of stock market taxation.

I am also immensely grateful to my **clients and students**—traders and investors who have trusted me with their tax planning and compliance needs. Your real-world challenges and queries inspired me to simplify complex tax concepts in this book.

A heartfelt appreciation goes to my **editor, reviewers, and publishing team** for their meticulous efforts in refining and structuring this book, ensuring that it delivers maximum value to readers.

Lastly, thank **you, the reader**, for picking up this book and investing in your financial knowledge. It empowers you to navigate tax compliance with confidence and optimize your trading and investment journey.

This book is dedicated to **every trader and investor striving for financial success while staying tax-compliant.** May it be a valuable resource in your journey beyond the trades!

With deepest gratitude,

CA Pankaj Himthani

DISCLAIMER

The information provided in this book, **"Tax Secrets Beyond the Trades,"** is for educational and informational purposes only. While every effort has been made to ensure the accuracy and reliability of the content, tax laws and financial regulations are subject to change. Readers are encouraged to consult with a **qualified Chartered Accountant, tax professional, or financial advisor** before making any tax or investment decisions.

The author, **CA Pankaj Himthani**, and the publishers do not assume any responsibility for errors, omissions, or any financial consequences arising from the use of the information in this book. The strategies, tax planning methods, and compliance guidelines discussed may vary based on individual circumstances, jurisdiction, and changes in tax laws.

This book does not constitute legal, tax, or financial advice. Any reliance placed on the material in this book is **strictly at the reader's discretion and risk**. The author and publisher shall not be held liable for any direct, indirect, or incidental damages resulting from the use or interpretation of this content.

By reading this book, you acknowledge and agree that you will seek professional advice tailored to your specific financial situation before acting on any tax-related or investment-related information.

All rights reserved. No part of this book may be reproduced, distributed, or transmitted in any form without prior written permission from the author or publisher.

difference in my tax burden. This is the guide I wish I had when I first started my business!

— Shoaib Dastgir, Entrepreneur

Foreword 3 – The Investor

As an investor, I knew that taxes played a crucial role in my overall returns, but I was never sure how to optimize them legally and efficiently. This book helped me navigate deductions, capital gains strategies, and tax-friendly investment vehicles with clarity. It's not just about making money—it's about keeping it! Highly recommended for any serious investor.

— Rahul Gallani, Stock Market Investor

Foreword 4 – The First-Time Taxpayer

When I started trading, I had no idea how to handle taxes. I was confused, frustrated, and worried about making mistakes. *Tax Secret Beyond the Trades* provided me with a step-by-step approach that made filing taxes stress-free and even beneficial. This book turned my fear into confidence, and I can't thank the author enough for that!

— Amit Kumar, New Trader & Freelancer

Foreword 5: Stock Market Trader Company

"I've tried other tax professionals in the past, but none have provided the level of expertise and personalized service that CA Pankaj Himthani offers. 'Tax Secrets Beyond the Trades' is a testament to their expertise, providing a clear and concise guide to tax strategy that is easy to understand and implement. I highly recommend this book to anyone looking to minimize their tax liability and maximize their returns."

— *Pradeep Sehrawat, Director*

TABLE OF CONTENTS

CHAPTER 1

INTRODUCTION OF TAXATION TO STOCK MARKET TRADERS & INVESTORS

"The Tax Raaz" - Unraveling the Mystery of Taxation for Stock Market Traders and Investors

In the bustling streets of Dalal Street, a young and ambitious trader, Rohan, had just made a killing in the stock market. His portfolio was flourishing, and his bank account was swelling. But, little did he know that his success had not gone unnoticed. He got the Notice and summon from the Income Tax Department, which made him vulnerable and anxious.

He Recalls his friend Mr. Niraj, whom he recently met at the conference, who was also actively trading in the stock market & doing very good with the finances.

Niraj introduced to Mr. Rajeev, A Chartered accountant who was India's Top Tax expert for stock market traders & investors.

Rohan scheduled a meeting with Mr. Rajeev to discuss the details of his journey and recent notices & summons from the IT department.

"Taxation is not just about paying taxes, my friend," Mr. Rajeev said. "It's about understanding the game, anticipating the moves, and making informed decisions."

Rohan's eyes widened as Mr. Rajeev unraveled the mysteries of taxation. He learned about the different types of taxes, deductions, and exemptions. He discovered the importance of maintaining proper records and documentation.

As Rohan's knowledge grew, so did his confidence. He began to make informed investment decisions, minimizing his tax liability and maximizing his returns.

But, Rohan's success was not without its challenges. He faced setbacks, losses, and even a tax audit. However, with Mr. Rajeev's guidance, he navigated each obstacle with ease.

"The tax raaz is not just about taxation," Mr. Rajeev said. "It's about discipline, patience, and perseverance."

Rohan's journey is a testament to the power of knowledge and planning. As a stock market trader or investor, you, too, can unlock the secrets of taxation and achieve success.

In this book, we will delve into the world of taxation for stock market traders and investors. We will explore the different types of taxes, deductions, and exemptions. We will discuss the importance of maintaining proper records and documentation.

By the end of this Book, you will have a clear understanding of the tax implications of your investment decisions. You will be equipped with the knowledge to make informed decisions, minimize your tax liability, and maximize your returns.

So, let's embark on this journey together. Let's unravel the mysteries of taxation and unlock the secrets of success.

Key Takeaways:

- Understanding the tax implications of stock market transactions

- Familiarity with tax laws and regulations governing stock market trading and investing

- Knowledge of different types of taxes applicable to traders and investors

- Awareness of tax deductions and exemptions available to traders and investors

- It is important to maintain proper records and documentation to support tax claims.

Taxation Basics for Stock Market Traders & Investors

"The Tax Tadka" - Spicing Up Your Tax Knowledge

"Tax Raaz 1: Types of Taxes"

"Rohan, there are two main types of taxes that apply to stock market traders and investors," said Mr. Rajeev. "Capital Gains Tax and Business Income Tax."

Rohan's eyes widened as Mr. Rajeev explained the difference between the two.

"Tax Raaz 2: Capital Gains Tax"

"Capital Gains Tax is applicable when you sell a security, such as a share or a mutual fund, for a profit," said Mr. Rajeev. "The tax rate depends on how long you held the security. If you hold it for less than a year, it's considered a short-term capital gain and is taxed at a higher rate. If you held it for more than a year, it's considered a long-term capital gain and is taxed at a lower rate."

Rohan nodded, taking mental notes.

"Tax Raaz 3: Business Income Tax"

"Business Income Tax is applicable when you trade in securities frequently, such as day trading or swing trading or F&O trading," said Mr. Rajeev. "In this case, your trading income is considered business income and is taxed accordingly."

Rohan's eyes sparkled with understanding.

"Tax Raaz 4: Tax Deductions & Exemptions"

"Rohan, there are several tax deductions and exemptions available to stock market traders and investors," said Mr. Rajeev. "For example, you can claim a deduction for brokerage charges or exchange charges or other legitimate expenses, or exemption of long-term capital gains from tax up to some few lacs rupees."

Rohan grinned, feeling empowered with his newfound tax knowledge.

"The Tax Tadka Takeaway"

"Rohan, my friend," said Mr. Rajeev, "taxation is not just about paying taxes; it's about understanding the tax tadka that comes with it. By knowing the tax basics, you can minimize your tax liability and maximize your returns."

Rohan nodded, feeling grateful for Mr. Rajeev's visit.

Key Takeaways:

- Understanding the two main types of taxes: Capital Gains Tax and Business Income Tax

- Knowing the tax rates and slabs for capital gains and business income

- Familiarity with tax deductions and exemptions available to stock market traders and investors

- Importance of maintaining proper records and documentation to support tax claims

CHAPTER #3

TAXATION ON CAPITAL GAINS

"The Capital Gains Saga" - A Taxation Tale

From Trump's Tweet to Elon's mail, Modi's Demonetization, GST implementation, COVID fall, or Putin-Ukraine war, Traders find all the ways to trade in Stock markets.

"Rohan, my friend," said Mr. Rajeev, " Capital City is divided into three kingdoms: Equity, Debt, and Mutual Funds, each with its tax laws.?"

"Tax Raaz 1: Equity "

"Equity investments, such as shares, are the heroes of the capital gains saga," said Mr. Rajeev. "They are taxed based on the holding period. If you sell your shares within 12 months, the gains are considered short-term capital gains (STCG) and are taxed at a flat rate of 20% w.e.f. 23rd July 2024. However, if you sell your shares after 12 months, the gains are considered long-term capital gains (LTCG) and are taxed at a rate of 12.50% for gains exceeding ₹1.25 lakh."

"Tax Raaz 2: Debt "

"Debt investments, such as bonds and debentures, are the villains of the capital gains saga," said Mr. Rajeev. "They are taxed based on the interest income earned. The interest income is taxed as per the tax slab rates. However, if you sell your debt investments, the gains are considered capital gains and are taxed accordingly to the individual slab rates."

"Tax Raaz 3: Mutual Funds "

"Mutual fund investments are the supporting actors of the capital gains saga," said Mr. Rajeev. "They are taxed based on the type of fund and the holding period. Equity-oriented mutual funds are taxed in the same way as equity investments. Debt-oriented mutual funds are taxed in the same way as debt investments."

Equity Mutual Funds:

- Taxation of STCG and LTCG is similar to equity shares.

- Equity-oriented mutual funds are mutual funds that invest at least 65% of their assets in equities and equity-related securities.

Debt Mutual Funds:

- Taxation of Debt Mutual funds is the same as that of debt instruments.

Rohan nodded, taking mental notes. Rohan grinned, feeling empowered with his newfound tax knowledge.

Key Takeaways:

- Understanding the taxation on capital gains on equity, debt, and mutual funds
- Knowing the tax rates and slabs for STCG and LTCG
- Familiarity with the tax exemptions and deductions available on capital gains

- Importance of maintaining proper records and documentation to support tax claims

CHAPTER 4

TAXATION OF BUSINESS INCOME

Once a Trader is always a Trader. Now, whether you love your spouse/GF/BF or not, you need to love your finances and capital more than them in order to trade in Stock Markets. So, protecting capital is so important in the markets. Taxation plays a major part in this Journey.

Rohan was taken aback by the taxation of Business Income from F&O and speculative transactions. He had never considered taxes beyond just paying them. Mr. Rajeev smiled and began to explain the taxation of business income for stock market traders and investors.

"Tax Raaz 1: Business Income - The Hero"

"Business income from F&O, Commodities, and other securities market derivatives are considered taxable income," said Mr. Rajeev. "It is taxed as per the tax slab rates, ranging from 10% to 30%."

"Tax Raaz 2: Trading Frequency - The Villain"

"However, if you trade frequently, you may be considered a trader rather than an investor," said Mr. Rajeev. In this case, your trading income is considered business income and is taxed accordingly." However, if you have invested in equities for more than 12 Months and are showing them as Investments, then you can show them as LTCG and pay reduced taxes.

"Tax Raaz 3: Speculative Transactions - The Supporting Actor"

"Speculative transactions, such as intraday trading in equity, are taxed separately," said Mr. Rajeev. "These transactions are considered speculative business income."

Taxation is the same as that of individual slab rate, but the treatment for Carried forward loss is separate.

Key Takeaways:

- Understanding the taxation on business income for stock market traders and investors
- Knowing the tax rates and slabs for business income
- Familiarity with the tax exemptions and deductions available on business income

- Importance of maintaining proper records and documentation to support tax claims

CHAPTER 5

TAXATION ON DIVIDEND INCOME

Over time, Rohan's admiration for Mr. Rajeev has only grown. With Mr. Rajeev's expert guidance, Rohan was able to navigate the intricacies of tax laws and regulations and ensure that his business was always compliant.

Whether you make money or lose money in the stock market, one thing is for sure: **TAXATION.** Remind me of the song:

"tu jahan jahan chale, tera saya"

Dividend income is free money, and nobody wants to leave it.

"Tax Raaz 1: Dividend Income "

"Dividend income is taxable in the hands of the recipient," said Mr. Rajeev. Currently, dividend income is added to the investor's total income and taxed according to their applicable income tax slab rates.

"Tax Raaz 2: Expenses of Dividend Income "

Investors can claim a deduction for interest expenses incurred to earn dividend income. However, this deduction is limited to 20% of the total dividend income.

Key Takeaways:

- Understanding the taxation on dividend income
- Knowing the tax rates and slabs for dividend income

- Familiarity with the tax exemptions and deductions available on dividend income

- Importance of maintaining proper records and documentation to support tax claims

CHAPTER 6

TAX DEDUCTIONS AND EXEMPTIONS &

TAX PLANNING STRATEGY

Looking back, Rohan can see that working with Mr. Rajeev had a lasting impact on his financial well-being. His guidance and expertise helped Rohan develop a deeper understanding of taxes and make informed decisions about my financial planning.

Trading in the stock market is like Whisky, and it gets better with age. So, as you grow in the markets, the more efficient and effective you need to be in Taxation, Said Mr. Rajeev.

"Expense Raaz 1: Brokerage Charges & Other Charges "

Brokerage charges & other charges such as GST, SEBI Fees, Stamp Duty, TOC NSE exchange, clearing charges & STT are like the entry fee to the stock market," said Mr. Rajeev. "You can claim all charges related to trading as a business expense, but only if you are trading frequently & Trading in F&O.

However, if you are not trading frequently or showing your income under Capital Gains, then all expenses except STT can be claimed as expenses.

"Expense Raaz 2: Internet and Mobile Expenses"

"Internet and mobile expenses are like the oxygen for your trading business," said Mr. Rajeev. "You can claim these expenses as a business expense or Capital Gain Selling expenses, but only if you use them exclusively for trading purposes or investment purposes, respectively."

"Expense Raaz 3: Office Rent and Utilities"

"Office rent and utilities are like the foundation of your trading business," said Mr. Rajeev. "You can claim these expenses as a business expense, but only if you use the office exclusively for trading purposes."

"Expense Raaz 4: Travel Expenses"

"Travel expenses are like the fuel for your trading business," said Mr. Rajeev. "You can claim travel expenses as a business expense, but only if you travel exclusively for trading purposes."

"Expense Raaz 5: Administration & Salary to Staff"

"Salary to staff such as trading floor staff, dealers, or admin staff are like the main pillars for your trading business," said Mr. Rajeev. "You can claim these expenses as a business expense or Capital Gain Selling expenses, but only if you use them exclusively for trading purposes or investment purposes, respectively.

"Expense Raaz 6: Consultancy or training expenses."

Mr. Rajeev said the trading world is everchanging and dynamic, so learning and development are part of it. You can claim Consultancy or Learning and development expenses as business expenses, as these are used exclusively for trading purposes.

"Expense Raaz 7: Information technology and software charges."

In this modern trading world, manual trading is not sufficient, so the use of algo trading and Artificial intelligence is a must," said Mr. Rajeev. You can claim these expenses as business expenses, as these are used exclusively for trading purposes.

Tax Planning Strategy:

1. Invest in tax-saving schemes: You can claim deductions under Section 80C by investing in ELSS, PPF, and other eligible schemes.

2. Claim exemptions: Claim exemptions for dividends, interest income, and capital gains from certain investments under Section 10.

3. Plan your investments: Plan your investments carefully to minimize your tax liability.

4. Maintain proper records: Maintain proper records and documentation to support your tax claims.

Key Takeaways:

- Understanding the business expenses allowed for stock market traders and investors
- Knowing the tax sections and rules
- Familiarity with the documentation required to support business expense claims
- Importance of maintaining proper records and documentation to support tax claims

COMPLIANCES AND REPORTING REQUIREMENTS

Rajeev's commitment to compliance and reporting has been a key factor in Rohan's success as a trader and investor. He has been a trusted partner and advisor, always available to provide guidance and support whenever Rohan needs it.

"Dalal Street ke sapne sach hote hain, Jab compliance aur integrity saath chalte hain!" Said Mr. Rajeev.

"Compliance Raaz 1: ITR Filing"

"ITR filing is like the grand finale of the compliance carnival," said Mr. Rajeev. "You need to file your income tax return (ITR) every year, disclosing your trading income and expenses & all other information related to investments."

"Compliance Raaz 2: Audit Requirements"

"Audit requirements are like the backstage pass to the compliance carnival," said Mr. Rajeev. "If your trading turnover exceeds ₹10 crore as of now, you need to get your accounts audited by a chartered accountant."

"Compliance Raaz 3: TDS Compliance"

"TDS compliance is like the ticket to the compliance carnival," said Mr. Rajeev. "You need to deduct tax at source (TDS) on certain payments, such as Salary, Consultancy, Professional fees, interest income, etc."

"Compliance Raaz 4: GST Compliance"

GST is not applicable to the securities market. However, if you have a business other than Securities trading, then GST compliance is like the grand entrance to the compliance carnival," said Mr. Rajeev. If you are trading in goods or services, you need to comply with the goods and services tax (GST) regulations."

"Compliance Raaz 5: SEBI Regulations and Exchange Rules"

Investors must adhere to the rules and regulations set by SEBI and the stock exchanges (NSE, BSE). These rules cover various aspects of trading, including order placement, settlement, and disclosure requirements. Some of the important areas are **KYC (Know Your Customer), Reporting of Transactions, Insider Trading Regulations, Market Manipulation - pump and dump.**

CHAPTER 8

SETOFF & CARRIED FORWARD PROVISION

As a trader and investor, Rohan had many fair shares of ups and downs. However, one of the most significant challenges Rohan faced was dealing with losses.

That's when Chartered Accountant Mr. Rajeev, stepped in and introduced me to the concept of carrying forward losses. Mr. Rajeev explained to Rohan that carrying forward losses can be a powerful tool for businesses for traders & Investors. By carrying forward losses, Rohan could offset them against future profits, reducing my tax liability and increasing my cash flow.

"Losses ko carry forward karne se aapke business ko fayda ho sakta hai." (Translation: "Carrying forward losses can benefit your business.") - Movie: Band Baaja Baaraat (2010) --- Said Mr. Rajeev.

"Setoff Raaz 1: Intra-Head Setoff"

"Intra-head setoff is like a magic trick that makes your losses disappear," said Mr. Rajeev. "You can set off losses from one trade against profits from another trade, as long as they are under the same head of income."

So, let's say you have a business other than a securities trading business. Then, you can set off with each other, or in layman's terms, the profit of one business can be nullified with the loss of another business.

"Setoff Raaz 2: Inter-Head Setoff"

"Inter-head setoff is like a puzzle that you need to solve," said Mr. Rajeev. "You can set off losses from one head of income against profits from another head of income, but only up to a certain limit." Generally, business losses (other than speculative business losses, *which is Intraday Equity Trading – this is discussed earlier*) can be set off against income from any other head of income, *except* salary income. Losses from speculative businesses (like intraday trading) can only be set off against profits from speculative businesses.

"Carry Forward Raaz 1: Losses from Business and Profession"

"Losses from business and profession are like a rainy-day fund that you can use in the future," said Mr. Rajeev. "You can carry forward losses from business and profession for up to 8 years and set them off against future respective business profits." So, business loss can be carried forward for

- **F&O Trading Losses**: Can be carried forward for up to **8 years**.

- **Intraday Trading Losses**: Can be carried forward for up to **4 years**.

"Carry Forward Raaz 2: Capital Losses"

"Capital losses are like a safety net that catches your falls," said Mr. Rajeev. "You can carry forward capital losses for up to 8 years and set them off against future capital gains."

Key Takeaways:

- Understanding the setoff and carried forward provisions for stock market traders and investors

- Knowing the intra-head and inter-head setoff rules

- Familiarity with the carry forward provisions for losses from business and profession and capital losses

- Importance of maintaining proper records and documentation to support setoff and carry forward claims

CHAPTER 9

CIRCULARS, CASE LAWS & JUDGMENTS

The iconic Sunny Deol dialogue *"Tareekh pe tareekh, tareekh pe tareekh milti gayi My Lord, par insaaf nahi mila."*

Referring to CBDT circular no. 6/2016 dated 29th February 2016 - Issue of taxability of surplus on sale of shares and securities - Capital Gains or Business Income.

There has always been a grey area in the taxation of short-term capital gain and business income.

Why?

STCG is currently taxed at 20%, whereas business income is taxable at the slab rates, which are a maximum of 30% with a surcharge.

Whether the surplus generated from the sale of listed shares or other securities would be treated as Capital Gain or Business Income shall take into account the following Pointer as per Circular: -

a) Where the assessee itself, irrespective of the period of holding the listed shares and securities, opts to treat them as stock-in-trade, the income arising from the transfer of such shares/securities would be treated as its business income.

b) In respect of listed shares and securities held for more than 12 months immediately preceding the date of its transfer, if the assessee desires to treat the income arising from the transfer thereof as Capital Gain, the same shall not be put to dispute by the Assessing Officer. However, this stand, once taken by the assessee in a particular Assessment Year, shall remain applicable in subsequent Assessment Years also, and the taxpayers shall not be allowed to adopt a different/contrary stand in this regard in subsequent years;

c) In all other cases, the nature of the transaction (i.e., whether it is capital gain or business income) shall continue to be decided, keeping in view the Circulars above issued by the CBDT.

As per the Author's view, if you have significant transactions, high frequency, and turnover in securities held less than 12 Months, then their income should be shown as Business Income. In simpler terms, the STCG should be combined with F&O profit and shown under "Profit and Loss

Account," and short-term equity Holding should be shown under Stock-in-trade.

However, Long-term Equity holdings, which are held for more than 12 months, can be shown under LTCG.

Several judicial pronouncements have provided clarity on various aspects of such taxation. Here are some notable case laws:

1. **Classification of Income: Business Income vs. Capital Gains**

- **Gargi Traders Pvt. Ltd. vs. Department of Income Tax**:

In this case, the Income Tax Appellate Tribunal (ITAT) observed that the taxpayer consistently maintained separate portfolios for shares held as stock-in-trade and those held as investments. The income from the sale of shares held as stock-in-trade was offered as business income, while income from shares held as investments was offered as capital gains. The tribunal upheld this bifurcation, emphasizing the importance of the taxpayer's intent and consistency in classification.

- **Smt. Yamini Khandelwal vs. Income Tax Officer (2022):**

The Kolkata Income Tax Appellate Tribunal (ITAT) addressed whether income from the sale of shares and mutual funds should be classified as business income or capital gains. The taxpayer, engaged in derivative trading, reported gains from share transactions as capital gains. The Assessing Officer reclassified these as business income, citing the high volume of transactions and the use of borrowed funds. The Tribunal ruled in favor of the taxpayer, stating that a high volume of transactions and the utilization of borrowed funds alone do not necessarily indicate business income. The taxpayer's consistent treatment of these transactions as investments in previous years was also a factor in the decision.

- **Rakesh Kumar Gupta vs. Income Tax Officer (2017):**

The Delhi ITAT considered the case of a taxpayer engaged in frequent trading of quoted shares. The Assessing Officer categorized the income as business income due to the high frequency and volume of transactions. The Tribunal upheld this view, noting that the taxpayer's substantial turnover and regularity in transactions indicated a trading motive rather than investment intent. This case underscores the significance of transaction frequency, volume, and the taxpayer's intent in classifying income from share transactions.

2. Set-off of Share Trading Losses Against Other Income

- **Share Trading Losses and Salary Income:**

In a case highlighted by CaseMine, the court noted that income tax provisions do not permit the set-off of share trading losses against salary income. This underscores the importance of correctly categorizing income and understanding permissible set-offs under the Income Tax Act.

3. Deductibility of Securities Transaction Tax (STT)

- **Deduction under Section 36 of the Income Tax Act:**

Section 36 allows for the deduction of STT paid, provided the income from the sale of securities is considered business income. However, if such income is treated as capital gains, STT is not deductible as a cost of acquisition. This distinction is crucial for taxpayers when determining the deductibility of STT.

TAKE THE NEXT STEP IN OPTIMIZING YOUR TRADING PROFITS

Option 1: Schedule A Webinar Session

If you're interested in learning more about how to optimize your trading profits and reduce your tax liability, I regularly Conduct an educational webinar. Together, we'll review Tax strategy and identify areas for improvement. Below is the link to the scheduling for the webinar:

https://calendly.com/pankaj-himthani

or scan the QR code to connect with me on various Social Media platform:

★ ★ ★

Option 2: Join Our Exclusive Trading Community

Join our exclusive trading community, where you'll gain access to:

- Exclusive trading insights and analysis
- Regular updates on tax laws and regulations
- Opportunities to connect with other traders and investors

- Access to our library of trading resources and tools

By joining our community, you'll be able to stay ahead of the curve and optimize your trading profits.

"Don't Miss Out on This Opportunity to Transform Your Trading Business"

To get the schedule for webinar or join our exclusive trading community, visit our website:

[www.capankajh.com] or email us at

[capankajhimthani@gmail.com]

We look forward to helping you achieve your trading goals!

MAY I ASK YOU FOR A SMALL FAVOR?

First, I want to thank you for reading this book. You could have chosen any other book, but you took mine, and I appreciate this. I hope you have at least a few actionable insights that will positively impact your daily life.

Can I ask for 30 seconds more of your time?

I'd love it if you could leave a review of the book. That will help me grow my readership by encouraging folks to take a chance on my books.

Keeping it straight - *reviews are the lifeblood of any author.*

It will take less than a minute of your time but will tremendously help me reach out to more people.

If you liked this book, ***please consider posting an honest review on your preferred retailer. And I'd love to see your review.***

Thanks for your support.